Did you enjoy this notebook?

Thank you for the purchase. We'd love to hearing your feedback, opinions and advice. So we would appreciate it, if you left a review.

Thank You :)

Travel Journal Publishers

This book belongs to:

_____

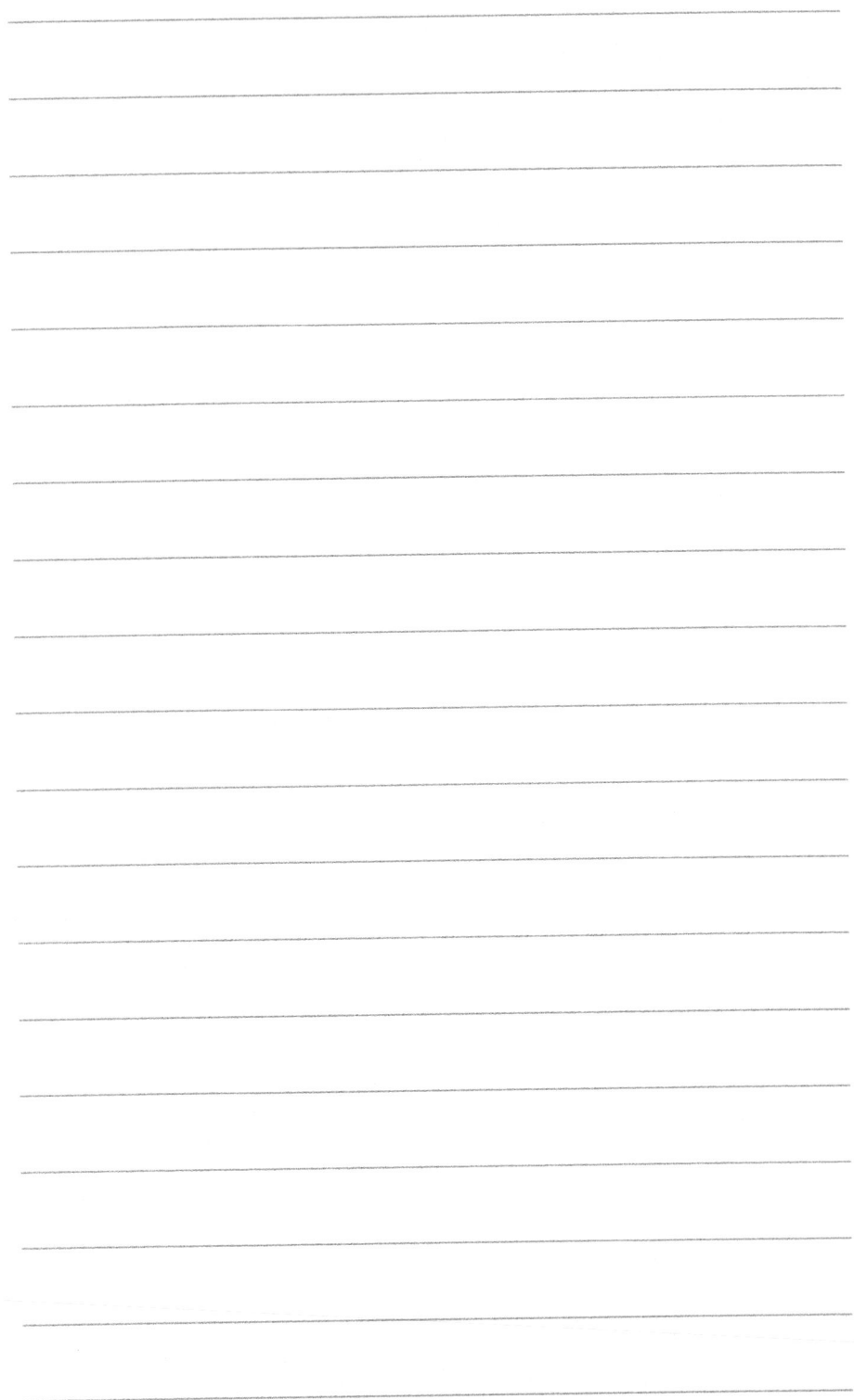

Made in the USA
Monee, IL
29 May 2023